What Do Pliers Do?

by Robin Nelson

first step nonfiction

Lerner Publications Company · Minneapolis

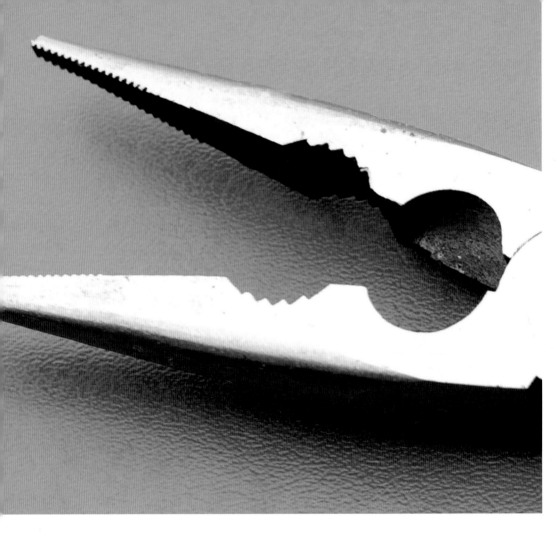

What tool is this?

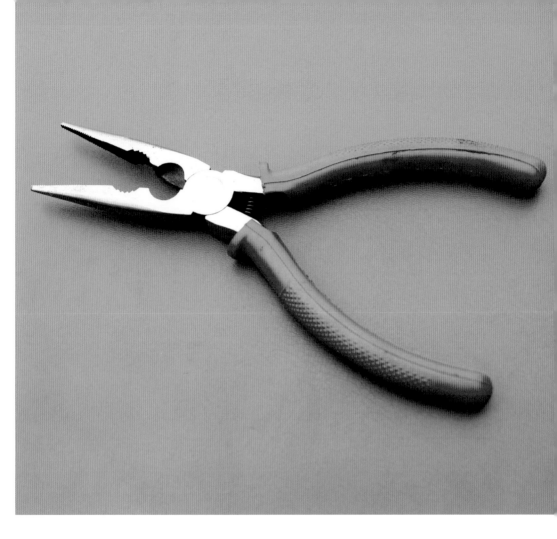

These are pliers.

Tools help us do jobs.

Pliers make jobs easier.

Pliers help us **grip** things.

Grip means "to hold tightly."

These are the **jaws** of the pliers.

The jaws grip things.

The jaws have teeth.

The teeth keep objects from
slipping.

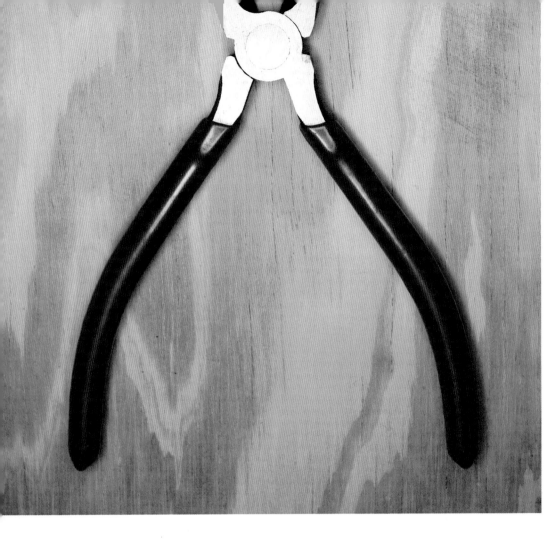

These are the handles.

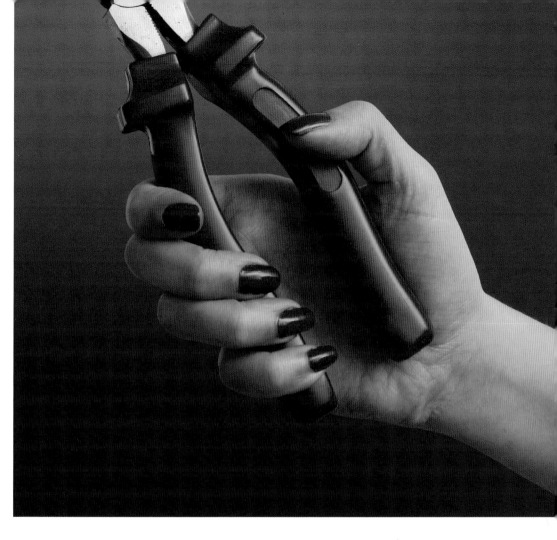

We press the handles
together to grip things.

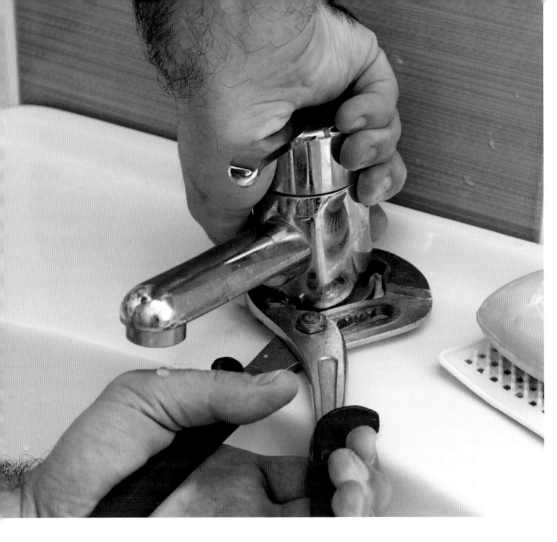

A plumber fixes a leaky
sink with pliers.

Electricians use pliers to twist and fix wires.

People use pliers to make jewelry.

What can you do with pliers?

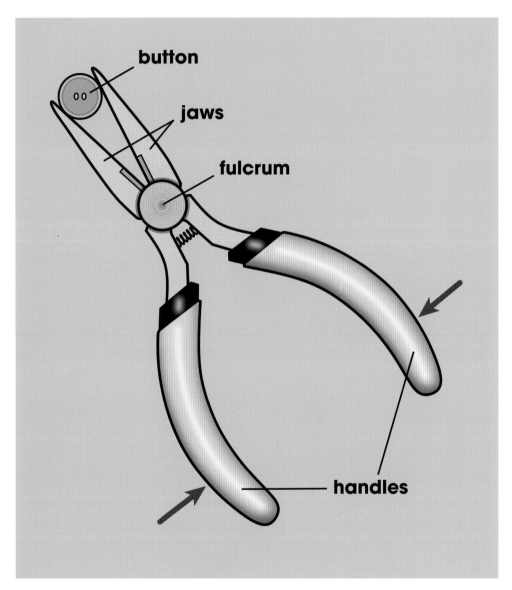

button

jaws

fulcrum

handles

Pliers Are Levers

Pliers are simple machines. They are **levers**. A lever is a strong bar. People use levers to move or hold things. The bar moves back and forth or up and down on a point called a **fulcrum**. You push on one end of the bar, and the other end moves an object.

The handles on pliers are two levers. Pick up a button by squeezing the pliers' handles. The handles act as levers. The jaws push together to hold the button.

Safety First

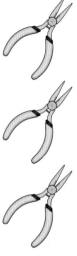

Ask a grown-up to help before using any tools.

Wear safety glasses to protect your eyes.

Roll up your sleeves. Tuck in your shirt. Tie back your hair. Take off any jewelry that might get in the way.

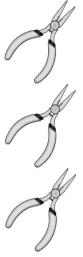 Never run with a tool in your hand.

Be careful not to pinch your fingers.

Put away the pliers when you are done with your job.

Glossary

electricians – people who work on electrical things

fulcrum – the point where a lever moves

grip – to hold something tightly

jaws – part of the pliers that open and close to hold something

levers – strong bars that are used to move something

Index

The images in this book are used with the permission of: © zhaoliang70/Shutterstock.com, pp. 2, 3; © donatas1205/Shutterstock.com, p. 4; © Hisham Ibrahim/Photodisc/Getty Images, p. 5; © Todd Strand/Independent Picture Service, pp. 6, 17; © Viesturs Kalvans/Dreamstime.com, pp. 7, 22; © Easyshoot/Dreamstime.com, pp. 8, 22; © iStockphoto.com/Igor Smichkov, p. 9; © Manfredxy/Dreamstime.com, p. 10; © luchunyu/Shutterstock.com, p. 11; © iStockphoto.com/ Sawayasu Tsuji, p. 12; © iStockphoto.com/Jimena Brescia, p. 13; © iStockphoto.com/Fuego, p. 14; © Image Source/Getty Images, pp. 15, 22; © iStockphoto.com/esolla, p. 16; © Laura Westlund/Independent Picture Service, pp. 18, 20, 21, 22.

Front cover: © Todd Strand/Independent Picture Service.

Main body text set in ITC Avant Garde Gothic Std Medium 21/25.
Typeface provided by Adobe Systems.

Lerner Publications Company
A division of Lerner Publishing Group, Inc.
241 First Avenue North
Minneapolis, MN 55401 U.S.A.

Website address: www.lernerbooks.com

Library of Congress Cataloging-in-Publication Data

Nelson, Robin, 1971–
     What do pliers do? / by Robin Nelson.
         p.   cm. — (First step nonfiction–tools at work)
   Includes index.
     ISBN 978–0–7613–8980–4 (lib. bdg. : alk. paper)
     1. Pliers—Juvenile literature. I. Title.
   TJ1201.T65N45 2013
   621.9'92—dc23   2011039075

Manufactured in the United States of America
1 – CG – 7/15/12